MW00934194

PENY'S PURSE

PENY'S PURSE

A True Story of a
Determined and
Brave Woman

Written by
Natalie Elliott
Illustrated by Naomi Davis

gatekeeper press
Where Authors are Family
Columbus, Ohio

The views and opinions expressed in this book are solely those of the author and do not reflect the views or opinions of Gatekeeper Press. Gatekeeper Press is not to be held responsible for and expressly disclaims responsibility of the content herein.

Peny's Purse: A True Story of a Determined and Brave Woman

Published by Gatekeeper Press
2167 Stringtown Rd, Suite 109
Columbus, OH 43123-2989
www.GatekeeperPress.com

Copyright © 2020 by Natalie Elliott
All rights reserved. Neither this book, nor any parts within it may be sold or reproduced in any form or by any electronic or mechanical means, including information storage and retrieval systems without permission in writing from the author. The only exception is by a reviewer, who may quote short excerpts in a review.

The cover design for this book is entirely the product of the author. Gatekeeper Press did not participate in and is not responsible for any aspect of this element.

Library of Congress Control Number: 2020942879

ISBN (hardcover): 9781662903304
ISBN (paperback): 9781662903311
eISBN: 9781662903328

To my Aunt Peny - whose hilarious and feisty personality,
love for animals, learning, and family will never be forgotten.

"HAHAHA!" Peny's infectious laugh echoed throughout Arnold's Restaurant. She laughed with her entire soul, the kind that was rooted in her stomach with her whole mouth wide open. It was a beautiful, warm July afternoon in Long Beach, California. She was enjoying lunch with her nieces Monique, Natalie, and Jasmine, and nephews Michael, Patrick, Jonathan, Ellis, Ryan, and Matthew.

Peny was a loyal Arnold's Restaurant customer. She rarely deviated from her traditional order – spaghetti and meatballs. She loved treating her nieces and nephews to meals out, especially on Mondays to capitalize on the "lunchtime special." One child, per adult, could eat lunch for free that day. A **free** meal? Score!

Although she loved a delicious family lunch, Peny relished a good financial deal even more. Saving money, even pennies (no pun intended), was her jam. Her Pakistani parents taught her the value of a cent, causing her to live simply and frugally.

After lunch, Peny's family dropped her off at home. She continued that humble lifestyle as an elderly woman. She walked or rode the public bus everywhere because she never learned how to drive a car. Being non-materialistic, she lived in a modest house, too. She didn't care about modern upgrades or anything fancy at all. However, she did care about her house's outdoor landscape. It was always nicely mowed, bright green, and the flower beds gleamed in their orderly arrangement.

Walking up the red, Spanish-style steps to her front door, she noticed her mailbox was full. She grabbed the mail and steppedinside.

"Charles! Moses! Freddie! Where are you? It's time to eat!" she called. Peny had a naturally loud voice. What seemed like shouting to the average person was just her normal speaking volume.

"Meowwwwww," they replied in unison. The trio included Charlie, chubby and roly-poly-like; Moses, tender-looking, brown, and white; and Freddie, exotically ivory. The felines excitedly scurried into the kitchen, anxiously awaiting their now-late lunch. Although Peny was a gigantic animal lover, cats were always her favorite.

While Charles, Moses, and Freddie munched on their food, she browsed through her mail. Always wanting to save every cent, she hated receiving bills but was never late paying them. To Peny, there was nothing worse than paying that dreaded late fee.

Suddenly, she came across a letter from her favorite organization - the World Wildlife Fund! Although a true penny-saver, Peny had a hidden generous streak of spending money to save and protect animals.

Obsessed with cats and endangered animals, Peny frequently donated her time and money to local shelters and worldwide organizations that helped save these precious creatures. It bothered her that cruel adults hunted animals like giraffes, elephants, and wild cats. Shocking her bank account (and herself), she occasionally splurged on fancy blouses and sweaters that had intricate cats and giraffes embroidered on the fronts of the garments! She felt that wearing clothes like these might bring awareness to others.

Then, Peny started to think about the Earth without these animals. Extinct animals disrupt the life cycle for so many living things! A world without elephants? How weak! A world without cats? How could she survive? She had to do something.

Even though she was eighty years old, her age was not going to get in the way of her passion. But, how could **she** raise awareness? What could she do? At her age, she just couldn't travel anymore.

She began glancing around the room for ideas. There were typed labels for everything. She was so organized! Everything sure had its place.

Then, ding! An idea popped into her head. She could write letters to the President, convincing them to increase more funding for wildlife protection. She always loved reading and writing, but it had been so long since she'd written long essays and letters. She would need some help with it. So, she started thinking even deeper about how she was going to do this.

Peny was a fiercely independent woman her entire life. She always tackled things on her own and achieved her goals no matter what the size. Thinking back to her high school days in China, she excelled at the top of her class. But, one thing she never accomplished was graduating from college.

That's it! she thought. She could go back to school, refresh her essay writing skills, and then start helping animals by writing very convincing letters to the President!

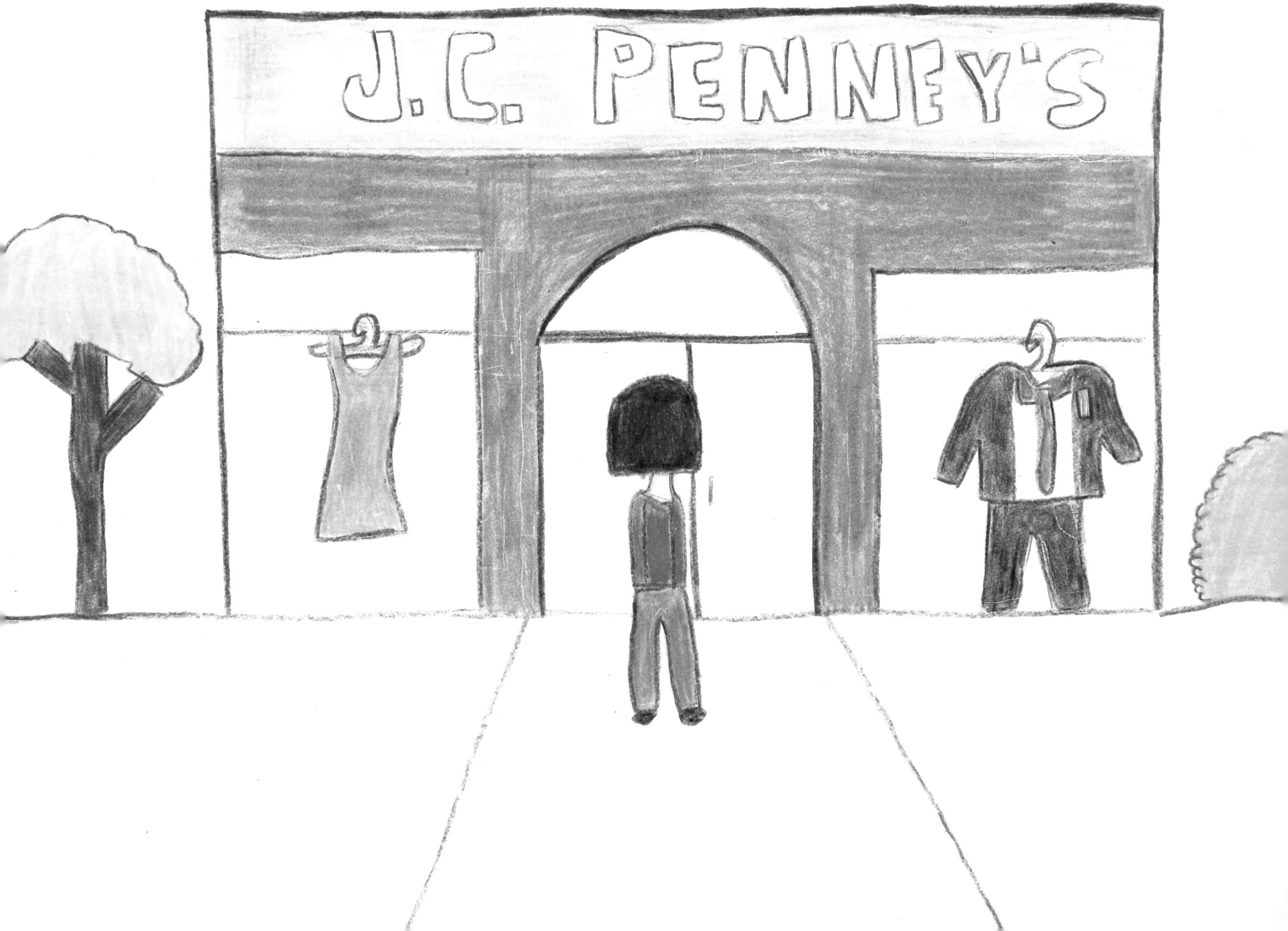
J.C. PENNEY'S

Immediately, she enrolled in the English Literature program at Cal State Long Beach. She couldn't wait to go back to school! To prepare, she decided she would visit J.C Penney to buy some professional clothes for this new learning adventure.

When she entered the store, the aroma of excessive perfume and cologne filled the air. The next moment, something caught her eye. It was large, square-shaped, shiny, black, and trimmed with gold zippers – a professional purse!

Peny, the penny-saver, had not purchased a new purse for fifteen years. This was the perfect time. She most certainly couldn't let the young folk outshine her scholarly comeback. She wanted both the students and the professors to take her seriously. **Just do it**, she persuaded herself. Something compelled her to buy it that day. **Little did she know that that black bag would play a big role in the future!**

Peny always adored school as a young girl. She attended school in China and was trilingual. She spoke English, Mandarin, and Russian.

At age eighty, she took three buses to Cal State Long Beach, carrying her black purse with her every time. At first, it was strange getting back into the routine of being a student again. After all, it had been quite a few decades!

Nonetheless, it wasn't too long before Peny emerged as a famous student on campus. The other students just loved her! From her infectious laugh and sarcastic personality to her endless intellect, she made friends with everyone. She soon proudly embraced the role of being the "old lady" with the black purse at school. She loved learning and taking classes!

Each day had a renewed purpose for Peny. She grew fond of getting ready for school, taking the bus to college with her new black purse, and chatting with the students and teachers. But most of all, she loved learning! Her writing skills were improving each day. She was hopeful that her words would definitely convince the President to protect the animals.

One morning, while walking home from school with her books and black purse, Peny noticed two men sitting in a car across the street from her house. She brushed it off and started walking up the red, Spanish-style steps to her black front door. When she took her keys out of her purse, she heard footsteps racing toward her.

A rush of different feelings flooded all over her! **What is happening? How many people are behind me? Why do I feel so scared right now? What do I do? Where are my neighbors? Help!**

Peny instantly thought to herself, **If I quickly get to the door, turn the key, lock the door, I can call the police**. But right after that thought crossed her mind, a split second later, she noticed they were almost right behind her! **I can't open the door. Who knows what they will do to my house!** she thought to herself, tucking the keys away in her purse.

Then, a moment later, she felt an ice cold hand cover her mouth.

The man told her she wouldn't get hurt if she gave him her purse. **Not my new black purse!** Peny was on the verge of tears. That purse had her school supplies in it and she **just** bought it.

She didn't have a choice. She released the purse out of her hand. The two naughty men grabbed it and started running away.

But, Peny's fierce, no-nonsense instincts were instantly triggered as she saw them escaping with her stuff. Throughout her life, she never let anyone boss her around, and she wasn't going to start now. She darted as fast as her old legs would allow, down the red steps, chasing after the car. Memorizing the car's license plate number, she immediately called the police.

"I've been robbed! Their plate number is N271922. They took my new black purse and school supplies! Please help!" she said in a shaky voice.

A few hours later, the police called Peny back with positive news. "Ma'am, we found the people who stole from you and took your black purse," the officer said calmly. Peny was so relieved. The police arrested them right away because they'd also robbed thirteen other elderly women that same day.

Several weeks after that horrible day, the police asked Peny to testify in court. That means she had to tell a judge what those mean people did to her. Peny did not want this to happen to any other woman. Plus, she wanted to show them that, even at eighty years old, she would be victorious!

So, she traveled to downtown Long Beach to give an honest statement of what happened. Thanks to Peny's overall determination and bravery, those naughty guys couldn't scare another lady again.

CAL STATE LONG BEACH

Months later, Peny continued her education. She worked hard, listened to her teachers, learned with her classmates, and improved her writing skills. She graduated with honors from Cal State Long Beach! Finally! She did it!

After graduating, with newly enhanced writing talents, Peny wrote countless letters to the President of the United States to encourage him to protect endangered animals. Since these animals couldn't voice their concerns for themselves, she made it her mission to help them. Because of her letters and donations, there have been many bills passed to protect animals from vanishing!

Peny is a true example that your age does not prevent you from accomplishing your goals or helping others. Live like Peny!

CPSIA information can be obtained
at www.ICGtesting.com
Printed in the USA
BVHW090123290920
589817BV00001B/1